BEING THERE
Tips for Supporting a Friend in Crisis

Leanne Currie-McGhee

San Diego, CA

© 2025 ReferencePoint Press, Inc.
Printed in the United States

For more information, contact:
ReferencePoint Press, Inc.
PO Box 27779
San Diego, CA 92198
www.ReferencePointPress.com

ALL RIGHTS RESERVED.
No part of this work covered by the copyright hereon may be reproduced or used in any form or by any means—graphic, electronic, or mechanical, including photocopying, recording, taping, web distribution, or information storage retrieval systems—without the written permission of the publisher.

LIBRARY OF CONGRESS CATALOGING-IN-PUBLICATION DATA

Names: Currie-McGhee, Leanne, 1971- author.
Title: Being there : tips for supporting a friend in crisis / by Leanne K. Currie-McGhee.
Description: San Diego, CA : ReferencePoint Press, Inc., 2025. | Includes bibliographical references and index.
Identifiers: LCCN 2024036200 (print) | LCCN 2024036201 (ebook) | ISBN 9781678210021 (library binding) | ISBN 9781678210038 (ebook)
Subjects: LCSH: Teenagers--Mental health--Juvenile literature. | Mentally ill teenagers--Care--Juvenile literature. | Crisis intervention (Mental health services)--Juvenile literature.
Classification: LCC RJ499 .C875 2025 (print) | LCC RJ499 (ebook) | DDC 618.92/89--dc23/eng/20240828
LC record available at https://lccn.loc.gov/2024036200
LC ebook record available at https://lccn.loc.gov/2024036201

CONTENTS

Introduction   4
Teens in Crisis

Chapter One   8
How Do I Recognize a Mental Health Crisis?

Chapter Two   17
Talking and Listening

Chapter Three   27
What Actions Can I Take?

Chapter Four   37
Reaching Out for Help

Chapter Five   45
Taking Care of Yourself While Helping Others

Source Notes   54
Getting Help and Information   57
Index   60
Picture Credits   64
About the Author   64

INTRODUCTION

Teens in Crisis

As you walk through the high school hallways, you greet friends and chat about classes, after-school plans, or the latest gossip. But sometimes, you might notice a classmate acting differently—maybe they're unusually quiet, unresponsive, or seem upset. It might be easy to brush it off as just a bad day, but what if it's more than that? What if they're struggling with anxiety, stress, or depression? Engaging with them could be the first step in helping them get the support they need. Reaching out might just be the lifeline they need.

Current Mental Health Crisis

Over the past decade, the mental health crisis among teens has reached alarming levels. Even before the COVID-19 pandemic, the number of teens experiencing mental health issues, self-harm, and attempted suicide was on the rise. The pandemic exacerbated these trends, leading to even higher levels of distress. According to the Centers for Disease Control and Prevention (CDC), in 2021 more than four in ten high school students felt persistently sad or hopeless, and nearly one-third experienced poor mental health. Additionally, more than one in five students seriously considered attempting suicide, and one in ten attempted suicide. CDC surveys indicate that certain groups, such as Black teens and LGBTQ youths, are at increased risk due to external pressures and negativity.

The factors contributing to this crisis are varied. Teens today face unprecedented pressures. While social media can offer connection, it also often heightens feelings of inadequacy and isolation. Academic expectations continue to rise, pushing teens to the brink of burnout. The COVID-19 pandemic further disrupted their lives, creating an environment of uncertainty, fear, and isolation without close social connections. This left many teens feeling overwhelmed and without the necessary coping mechanisms to manage their stress and mental health issues. Many needed help and did not know where to turn.

Why Peer Intervention Is Needed

A friend cannot cure another friend's mental health issues. Teens should understand the limits of what they can do—it is not their job, nor is it possible, for them to solve peers' problems. But a friend can be there to help and support in a time of need. Reasons that peer intervention is so important include the lack of mental health resources available to teens, the way teens respond openly to peers, and the fact that teens are likely able to discern changes in their friends that adults may not notice. That is why listening to your friends, suggesting professional help, and just letting them know you care for them are major ways to help.

The lack of easily available mental health resources for teens affects their ability to open up about any problems they are dealing with. For example, the shortage of school counselors is a significant issue nationwide. According to the American School Counselor Association, the average student-to-counselor ratio in the United States is 482 to 1, far exceeding the association's recommended 250 to 1 ratio. Since school is where most teens spend a majority of their time, this is the most accessible place for them to find help. But the disparity between the number of counselors needed versus available means that many students do not have immediate access to someone to talk to if they want to reach out for help.

When people don't have access to mental health resources, friends often become the first line of defense in recognizing and addressing mental health issues. For many teens, confiding in friends feels safer, less stigmatizing, and less intimidating than talking to adults. This peer-to-peer interaction can make a profound difference in the lives of those struggling with mental health challenges.

Peers are particularly effective because they are likely to notice changes in their friends' behavior, mood, or performance. "Typically, teens will confide in their friends when they are experiencing mental health struggles,"[1] says Vanessa Simpson, behavioral health care manager for a Texas pediatric health care system. These early observations can be crucial for timely intervention.

Consider Tara, who attends high school in Australia. She began to experience anxiety when her schoolwork increasingly became more challenging. She became distant and withdrawn from family and friends, and her anxiety deepened into depression. "The

No one can solve someone else's mental health problems, but listening, suggesting professional help, and letting them know you care are major ways to help.

situation started to get better when I finally began to open up about it," Tara says. "Suddenly, it didn't seem so bad after all. I opened up to a friend and, after all the tears and emotion, I realized that people did care about me. It was like a huge weight had been lifted from my shoulders."[2]

> "I opened up to a friend and, after all the tears and emotion, I realized that people did care about me. It was a like a huge weight had been lifted from my shoulders."[2]
>
> —Tara, high school student who suffered from depression

Knowing What to Do

Because of the potential impact peers can have on friends in need, health professionals feel it is important for teens to know how to spot symptoms of mental health problems. With this in mind, school districts in some states have begun teaching mental health first aid in schools. In 2023 eighteen high schools in New Jersey participated in a program run by the National Council for Mental Wellbeing in which students received training in how to recognize signs of mental health issues and provide initial help. This program emphasizes the importance of connection and equips teens with the skills to support each other. Lily Schulenberg, who took the course as a sophomore, says that it has helped her be more aware of others' mental health. "During the class, we were told, 'If you see something, say something,'"[3] she says. Teaching mental health first aid in schools not only empowers students but also fosters a culture of openness and support among teens.

Going Forward

The mental health crisis among teens continues to grow and needs to be addressed in many ways, according to mental health organizations. With the right support and education, peers can play a role in combating this crisis. They can help create a more supportive and understanding environment for their friends. Teens can show others that they are not alone in their struggles, and together, they can support and help one another.

CHAPTER ONE

How Do I Recognize a Mental Health Crisis?

Elaine Russell was in the seventh grade when she discovered that her best friend was cutting herself. The realization scared her, but she did not know this meant her friend was undergoing a mental health crisis. Not knowing how serious this was or what to do, Russell chose to ignore the situation at first. "As much as I pretended not to notice, I knew that she was struggling,"[4] Russell recalls. While worried, she kept quiet and did not say anything to her friend, her parents, her friend's parents, or anyone at all. Her friend ended up being admitted to the hospital for her cutting and self-harm. It was then that Russell realized the importance of recognizing the signs of a mental health crisis and knowing how to respond.

What Is a Mental Health Crisis?

A mental health crisis is any situation in which a person's behavior prevents them from being able to care for themselves or function effectively in their daily lives. It may even put them at risk of hurting themselves or others. For teens, these crises can take many forms and often involve extreme emotional distress.

Several types of mental health crises are common among teenagers, including anxiety, depression, eating disorders, and grief. The CDC found that in 2021, more than four in ten high school students reported feeling sad or hopeless.

Nearly a third experienced poor mental health, and this was most prevalent among LGBTQ, Black, and female students due to societal pressures and negative interactions with others. Additionally, grief and the challenges associated with significant life changes, such as a parent losing a job or dealing with a physical health issue, can lead to severe emotional distress. Vivek Murthy, then US surgeon general, issued a warning in 2021 that teens were experiencing a mental health crisis. He reported that suicide rates had gone up 57 percent from 2009 to 2019 among youths ages ten to twenty-four. While the causes behind these statistics are multifaceted, if a person is struggling, it is important to intervene no matter the cause.

It is critical to address such crises promptly to prevent long-term consequences. "The mental health of our children is crucial," writes Claire McCarthy, a primary care pediatrician at Boston Children's Hospital and an assistant professor of pediatrics at Harvard Medical School. "Not only does mental health affect physical health, but untreated mental health problems interfere with learning, socialization, self-esteem, and other important aspects of child development that can have lifelong repercussions."[5] Ignoring a mental health crisis can have severe impacts, including worsening symptoms, increased risk of self-harm or suicide, academic decline, and strained relationships. Timely intervention can make a significant difference in a teen's recovery and overall well-being. For this reason, it is important for teens to understand what behaviors can indicate a mental health crisis.

> "Not only does mental health affect physical health, but untreated mental health problems interfere with learning, socialization, self-esteem, and other important aspects of child development that can have lifelong repercussions."[5]
>
> —Claire McCarthy, a primary care pediatrician at Boston Children's Hospital and an assistant professor of pediatrics at Harvard Medical School

Know the Signs

There are some common signs of someone experiencing emotional distress. Physical changes are typically the most visible indicators

Anxiety disorders and other mental health problems are common among teens, with nearly one-third reporting issues.

that something is wrong. These can include sudden and unexplained changes in weight, recurring pains such as headaches or stomach pain, and constant tiredness.

Sudden and unexplained weight changes can be a significant red flag. If you notice that a friend's weight is fluctuating a lot or that he or she has changes in appetite, whether increased or decreased, these can signal mental health concerns. If someone suddenly loses interest in food or starts eating significantly more than usual, it might be the person's way of coping with emotional distress. Rapid weight loss might indicate severe stress, anxiety, or depression, while rapid weight gain can be associated with emotional eating or other coping mechanisms. Both can have serious implications for a person's physical and mental health. Additionally, these changes may be a sign of an eating disorder, another type of mental health issue.

Constant tiredness and changes in sleep patterns are also key indicators of mental health issues. If a friend is consistently exhausted, sleeping much more or less than usual, or experiencing insomnia, these could be signs of depression, anxiety, or other mental health conditions. Sleep is closely linked to mental health, and sleep disruptions can further exacerbate emotional and psychological difficulties. If the sleep issues are due to emotional stress, a cycle of disruptive sleep can develop that makes the emotional problems seem even more daunting.

Additionally, unexplained physical complaints—such as frequent headaches, stomachaches, or other aches and pains—can sometimes be linked to mental health issues. These symptoms can result from stress, anxiety, or depression, especially when there is no apparent physical cause. Understanding these physical signs is crucial for recognizing when a friend might be struggling with their mental health.

Behavioral Changes

Behavioral changes are also crucial indicators of a mental health crisis. According to the American Psychological Association, the most common indication of mental health issues is any abrupt change in behavior. Sudden changes in temperament, social interactions, or personality, such as becoming more aggressive or irritable, can be a sign of emotional distress.

Not everyone experiences depression or anxiety in the same way, and symptoms can vary. However, there are certain behaviors that a person going through a tough time may exhibit. According to ReachOut, a nonprofit organization in Australia dedicated to improving youth mental health, "If your friend is experiencing depression, they might seem down or tearful a lot of the time, or cranky more often, stay up really late or sleep in a lot, or have problems with sleep, miss a lot of school, work or their regular activities, or miss hangouts or often cancel at the last minute."[6]

Specific actions to look for are when your friends stop engaging in activities they typically enjoy or are invested in. For example,

Trust Your Gut

It is hard to decide to intervene in a friend's life if they have not asked for help or talked about mental health struggles. But professional mental health organizations emphasize that a significant number of people struggling do not actively ask for help. For this reason, teenagers should trust their instincts if they have a feeling that something is wrong. "You know your friend, and when you notice signs that make you think that your friend is struggling, your gut may tell you that they need help. In moments like these it's important to follow your instincts, even if you aren't totally sure they are right on," recommends the Jed Foundation, a nonprofit organization dedicated to protecting the mental health of teenagers and young adults.

Friends know how other friends act and behave, so ultimately, they are likely to notice a difference in another friend's behavior. If you see a difference, acting on it may ease your friend's struggle and in some cases may save his or her life.

Jed Foundation, "How to Follow Your Instincts When You're Worried About a Friend." https://jedfoundation.org.

---

some teens who are depressed may stop attending social activities or sports or putting effort into their classes. Behavioral changes may also include a sudden drop in grades or frequent absences from school. Daneisha Carter experienced extreme anxiety when she was eighteen and recalls how it affected her ability to keep up with her daily life. "As time went on, it felt like my anxiety was getting worse and worse. I became very stressed out. I started losing focus on school, work, everyday tasks, and I had personal issues at home I was battling,"[7] Carter explains.

Also, how peers react to others, including friends, is something to look out for. If they are persistently irritable with others, this could be an indicator that something is wrong. Increased secrecy or withdrawal from family and friends are other red flags. Teens might start spending more time alone, avoiding interactions, or becoming unusually secretive about their activities and feelings. These behaviors can indicate that they are struggling to cope with their emotions.

Another behavioral sign is a decline in personal hygiene. When someone stops taking care of their appearance, it might reflect their internal struggle. Neglecting basic grooming—like showering, brushing teeth, or changing clothes regularly—can be a sign that a person is feeling overwhelmed or too fatigued to maintain his or her usual routines.

Cooper Devine, a senior in Wisconsin in 2024 and a member of Hope Squad, a school-based suicide prevention group, has learned about and used his understanding of emotional distress signals to help others. "Sometimes it is me reaching out to someone I see is struggling," says Devine. "Maybe I see them and they're acting different than they usually do, and I don't know what that means. So I ask them about it."[8] Understanding the signs can give peers the ability to be proactive in reaching out and offering support.

> "Maybe I see them and they're acting different than they usually do, and I don't know what that means. So I ask them about it."[8]
>
> —Cooper Devine, a senior in high school and member of Hope Squad

Sudden changes in temperament, social interactions, or personality, such as becoming withdrawn or sad all the time, can be a sign of emotional distress.

Paying Attention

Recognizing when a friend is struggling emotionally isn't always straightforward, because changes can occur gradually and may not immediately appear to be severe. Also, it is not always easy to tell what the signs actually mean. For instance, unexpected bouts of anger could indicate underlying depression, while isolation might signal anxiety. Or withdrawing from activities or friends could actually be linked to an eating disorder. It's important to use these observations not to diagnose your friend but rather to realize that they might be going through something challenging and could benefit from your support. This awareness becomes particularly important if the signs go beyond a day or so. Being attentive to these behaviors can let you know whether it is time to intervene. Taking proactive steps to acknowledge and respond to these signs can create an environment where your friend feels understood and cared for during difficult times.

Additional Clues

Other types of clues, some of which are fairly subtle, can indicate a mental health crisis. These include verbal and nonverbal clues such as statements of distress, changes in how a friend is (or is not) communicating with you, and a noticeable shift toward withdrawal.

Verbal cues might include expressions of hopelessness, with your friends saying things like "I can't do this anymore" or "What's the point?" These statements can indicate a sense of hopelessness and a lack of motivation about activities and daily life they used to enjoy. It's important to listen carefully to the language your friends use, as these expressions might reveal their inner struggles. Other phrases such as "I'm tired all the time" or "Nothing matters anymore" can also be significant indicators of emotional distress like depression or anxiety. Taking these verbal cues seriously and learning how to respond with empathy and support can make a crucial difference in helping your friends feel understood and less isolated.

Nonverbal cues can also show a friend's emotional state. These may include avoiding eye contact, sudden silence, or reluctance to engage in conversations. A noticeable shift toward withdrawal might occur, and you may notice a friend who once actively participated in group chats or social media becoming unusually quiet or completely disengaged. These subtle signs can often be the earliest indicators that something is wrong.

In 2023 thirteen-year-old Chantelle of London spoke on a video with Mind, a mental health charity in the United Kingdom. She has learned to notice when friends are not feeling emotionally well by observing their body language. For instance, she watches their actions during a conversation. "A lot of the information you can see from the eyes . . . if their eyes are down, and they're not really looking at you in the face, that could show a sense of anxiety, for they're nervous,"[9] she explains.

Janie Gorman also learned indicators to determine whether her friends or classmates are in emotionally stressful situations. In

> "A lot of the information you can see from the eyes . . . if their eyes are down, and they're not really looking at you in the face, that could show a sense of anxiety, for they're nervous."[9]
>
> —Chantelle, age thirteen, on mental health signs

Nonverbal cues, such as avoiding eye contact or reluctance to engage in conversations, can provide clues about a friend's emotional state.

2023 Gorman took a teen mental health first aid course at school. She, like every sophomore at Ramsey High School in Ramsey, New Jersey, was required to take a training program called Teen Mental Health First Aid, which is designed to give students the practical tools needed to recognize emotional crisis warning signs and know what to do. However, Gorman herself actually experienced a panic attack, a type of mental health crisis, and because her friends knew the signs from the same course, they were able to help her. She was out with her friends when she began to feel overwhelmed. Her fingers were tingling. She had trouble taking in a breath. She also felt dizzy and unsteady. Her friends noticed. They understood what the signs meant and knew to take action. "They immediately called my dad so he could talk to me. They found a water bottle for me," Gorman recalls. "They sat with me; they were just there for me."[10] Because they knew what to notice and how to respond, Gorman got the help she needed.

Time to Respond

Once you recognize that a friend may be in crisis, it is essential to take the next step and respond. Learning the most effective ways to help a friend or peer you think may be in crisis will help guide you to do what is best. According to the American Psychiatric Association, over a decade of research around the world has found that intervention can often minimize or delay symptoms, prevent hospitalization of individuals, and result in a more favorable outlook. Understanding and helping a friend in a mental health crisis can be challenging, but it is essential. By recognizing the signs of a crisis, once you learn how to respond, you can provide crucial support to your friends.

CHAPTER TWO

Talking and Listening

Deciding to engage with a friend who may be experiencing a mental health crisis is a significant and sometimes challenging decision. It is natural to feel uncertain, especially if you are not entirely sure whether your friend is in crisis. If you have observed concerning changes in your friend's behavior, it is usually better to engage than to ignore. Starting a conversation can open the way to helping them to get the support they need and potentially prevent the situation from worsening.

The reason it is important for peers to check in with their friends is that teens are more likely to open up to their friends about any emotional issues that they are experiencing. A 2022 study by the National Alliance on Mental Illness found that 65 percent of teens say they feel comfortable talking about their mental health with those who are closest to them. New Jersey Ottumwa High School counselor Kolby Streeby has observed that "friends are the first line of defense"[11] when students are having a hard time. Being willing to engage and offer support can be a lifeline to another. However, to be effective in this role, it is essential to be prepared and informed about how to approach and support someone in crisis.

Being Ready

One way to learn how to approach a peer is to take part in mental health support training courses offered at some schools. These programs give teens tools for handling these situations. Some people feel that teens are too young to handle the burden of helping friends with mental health struggles.

Suzanna Davis initially worried about this too. While a high school principal, she learned about a peer suicide prevention program called Hope Squad. She wondered whether students would find it burdensome. "But I realized they're having these conversations with their peers on a daily basis," she says. "In the absence of formal training, they very much carry the weight on their shoulders that they have to fix their friends' problems. If we're not engaging them and giving the right tools and training to engage in those conversations, we're missing the boat."[12] After retiring as a principal, she went to work for Grant Us Hope, a nonprofit organization that partners with Hope Squad to provide mental health training at 175 schools in Ohio and Indiana.

Hope Squad and similar programs focus on preventing suicide and promoting mental wellness. Participating students are taught to recognize the warning signs of suicide as well as who might be at risk. Some signs, such as teens who overtly threaten to hurt or kill themselves, are crystal clear. But other signs can be more subtle. Teens who make comments such as "I wish I would go to

Some high schools offer peer mental health support training courses. These courses give teens the knowledge, tools, and confidence to address potential mental health issues in others.

sleep and not wake up" or who are actively seeking out pills or a weapon could be signaling their intention to harm themselves. In situations like these, teens are taught to immediately contact the adults supervising their squads.

The squad members are also taught to recognize signs of stress and anxiety—and how to approach peers who are struggling with these emotions. If, for example, a friend suddenly stops going to softball practices or music lessons, you might want to ask whether everything is okay. Sometimes the student just needs someone to talk to in order to feel better. This might be the case if the friend was worried about a test or had an argument with a friend. But if the student talks about feeling depressed, especially if it has been going on for a while, this might call for speaking to a counselor or other adult in the program.

> "A lot of [the training] was how to recognize that somebody needs help and how to reach out to students who we thought could benefit from some sort of assistance from the counselor."[13]
>
> —Izabella Harju, Clark High School Hope Squad member

In 2022 Izabella Harju was a member of the Hope Squad at Clark High School of Nevada. She said their ability as peers to understand the issues of other teens combined with their training allows squad members to confidently approach other students. "We did go through a pretty long training process. . . . A lot of [the training] was how to recognize that somebody needs help and how to reach out to students who we thought could benefit from some sort of assistance from the counselor."[13] She added that an important part of the training was to listen to peers to show them that they are safe and can trust you.

How to Approach

When approaching a friend or peer who you think may be experiencing mental distress, it is crucial to create a supportive and safe environment. This involves practicing empathy, being nonjudgmental, maintaining confidentiality, and understanding how to convey these attitudes effectively. Before talking with a friend, plan on coming to the conversation with these attitudes.

Online Support

Teens in parts of Nevada and Kansas who are dealing with emotional issues such as stress and loneliness have the opportunity to connect online with teens who are experiencing similar feelings. They can do so through an online chat service focused on peer mental health support. This pilot program is provided by Supportiv, a virtual peer-to-peer support system, and UnitedHealthcare, a health insurance company. To access the chat service, students can visit the Supportiv website. The website asks simple questions about what they are experiencing. Some teens might say they are overwhelmed by homework or lonely at school. Other teens have other concerns. The program uses their answers to match them with chat groups whose members are undergoing similar challenges.

Professionally trained moderators guide these chats, balancing opportunities for teens to vent their frustrations and learn how to move forward in positive ways. The moderators also keep the chats focused on coping, healing, and problem-solving skills. "Our moderators do more than just listen. They are trained to facilitate the conversations to not only keep students safe, but to reduce sadness, anger, loneliness, and stress, while improving overall optimism," says Helena Plater-Zyberk, co-founder and CEO of Supportiv. The service is available around the clock and is free of charge. All interactions are anonymous.

Quoted in UnitedHealthcare, "Anonymous Peer Support Helps Cultivate Youth Mental Health," April 22, 2024. www.uhc.com.

Empathy is the ability to understand and share the feelings of another. Empathy is essential when supporting a friend who is struggling. It allows you to develop trust. When you show empathy, you validate your friend's feelings and experiences, which can be incredibly comforting. According to Brené Brown, a research professor of social work at the University of Houston, "Empathy is feeling WITH people. I always think of empathy as this kind of sacred space. When someone's in a deep hole and they shout from the bottom and they say 'I'm stuck. It's dark. I'm overwhelmed.' and we look and we say 'Hey' and climb down and say 'I know what it's like down here, and you're not alone.'"[14] Major components of empathy are actively listening to your friend without interrupting and acknowledging their emotions without trying to immediately fix the problem. This helps your friend feel heard and understood, which is often the first step toward healing.

Closely tied to empathy is being nonjudgmental. It involves accepting your friends' feelings and experiences without making them feel criticized or ashamed. You want to ensure that they feel there is no stigma attached to needing emotional help. One way to do this is with reflective listening. This is when you repeat back what they've said in your own words, instead of asking them why they feel a certain way. For example, you might say, "It sounds like you're feeling really overwhelmed with everything going on." This type of statement shows that you are trying to understand their perspective without judgment. When friends feel they are not being judged, they are more likely to open up and share their true feelings.

Confidentiality is when you let your friend know that you will not disclose anything they share with you without their permission. This is necessary for building trust. Your friend needs to know you can keep a secret, except in situations when their safety or the safety of others might be at risk. Mental health professionals suggest setting clear expectations and boundaries up front. Let your friend know that you are there to listen and offer support and that you will not divulge what they tell you unless you feel they may be in danger. Tell them that in such a case, you will need to involve a trusted adult.

Nonverbal language can also help convey your intentions. Mental health professionals advise paying close attention to your friend, maintaining eye contact, and responding with nods or brief affirmations to show you are engaged. Avoid distractions, such as checking your phone, to show you are invested in what they are saying and how they are feeling. By setting the right tone, you can create a supportive environment that encourages friends to share their struggles and seek the help they need.

Engaging a Peer

Starting a conversation with a friend who is struggling can be difficult. Sometimes it's hard to know what to say. The first consideration is choosing the right environment for such a conversation. Try to avoid bringing up serious matters in busy public spaces like a school classroom or at a school event with many students. Instead, select a private and comfortable space where both of you can speak openly without distractions. This could be a quiet corner in a coffee shop, a park bench outside, or a room where you know you won't be interrupted.

To initiate the conversation, you can use simple and honest conversation starters that demonstrate your concern based on your observations. For example, you might say, "I've noticed you've been really quiet lately. Are you feeling okay?" or "I've noticed you haven't been coming to soccer practices. Do you want to talk about it?" These openers show that you care and have been paying attention to them, without being judgmental or too intrusive.

When you do talk, it is crucial to be direct and honest. Ask questions that encourage the sharing of feelings without pushing

Choose a quiet, private spot for serious conversations with a friend so you can speak openly without distractions or the fear of being overheard.

Keep It Casual

Beginning a conversation with a friend about mental health doesn't mean you have to dive straight into talking about any type of struggles or have an intense conversation. This is the central message of Seize the Awkward, a national public service campaign that encourages teens and young adults to reach out to friends who may be experiencing difficulties. The campaign's website provides conversation starters and suggestions for how to approach friends. It also features videos of celebrities explaining their own mental health challenges and the impact of talking about mental health issues with their friends, as well as promoting the idea of finding a safe, casual space for such conversations. This can mean grabbing a bite to eat after class, going on a walk, or even playing a game of basketball. Then, one way to start a conversation is to bring up something that's troubling you, which would give your friend an opening to mention their own struggles. Or, if you game with them online, set up a game and then you can reach out in the DMs to them during the game. No matter how you do it, the purpose is to make contact with that friend, and in a situation where they can feel comfortable connecting with you.

too hard. Kathryn Gordon, a clinical psychologist in North Dakota, emphasizes the importance of asking open-ended questions. "Ask simple follow-up questions like, 'What does that feel like?' or 'What has been on your mind as you're going through this?'"[15] These types of questions will give your friends the space to open up. Listening attentively is key. Ask follow-up questions to help them more fully express their emotions and experiences.

Being There

Sometimes it's hard to know for certain whether a friend is suffering. If your observations tell you there's a problem and your instinct—or gut feeling—tells you there's a problem, don't ignore it. Approaching a friend with the right attitude and words can be difficult, but it can also be lifesaving. Remi Cruz, a well-known YouTuber and podcaster, discovered this recently. She knew that she needed to talk to a friend who was showing signs of mental

YouTuber Remi Cruz, who has spoken out about how to help friends experiencing mental health crises, appears at the 2022 Billboard Women in Music Awards in Los Angeles, California, on March 2, 2022.

health issues. "I have a very close personal friend in my life who has struggled for the past four years or so with extreme anxiety, depression, suicidal thoughts, and things like that," Cruz explains. "I kind of noticed something was different when they just started acting a little bit strange, a little bit out of the ordinary."[16]

Cruz decided to talk her friend to see whether she could get the friend to open up. The two were at the friend's house. The friend was lying outside on a mattress, acting withdrawn and out of sorts. Cruz sat down next to her friend. Cruz recalls:

> I just asked like what's going on? Are you okay? What's happening? Like this isn't normal. And that night was the night that they were actually, like had extreme suicidal thoughts, and I had no idea. I didn't know that they were feeling this way for so long, and they just kept it bottled in. Asking them was definitely uncomfortable, especially because I didn't want to offend them in any way. I didn't want to make them feel like they weren't validated. That's a really big thing, I think. And it's an uncomfortable thing for sure, but it's something that needs to be done, too.[17]

Cruz ended up sharing her friend's suicidal thoughts with the friend's family, and they were able to intervene. Today her friend is on medication, is in therapy, and has a community of supportive friends and family. Cruz is thankful she noticed her friend's behavior and engaged with the friend. She is also grateful that her friend felt comfortable enough to talk about what was going on. Cruz encourages others to follow their instincts when concerned about someone.

> "I just asked like what's going on? Are you okay? What's happening?"[17]
>
> —Remi Cruz, YouTuber, approaching a struggling friend

Following Up

After initiating a conversation with a friend you're concerned about, it is crucial to keep the lines of communication open. Liza Koshy, a twenty-year-old actress, and her friend opened up to each other about their struggles. They also devised a way to check in with one another. Koshy explains:

> I have a friend who opened up to me about his OCD and it was something that was very tough for him to open up about because he had never opened up to anybody about

it before. And I completely related to that because I had been holding in my feelings about my anxiety for an entire year. It just started this free-flow of conversation between both of us about my anxiety, about his OCD, about these two things that we didn't know about each other. . . . Now we actually have a code name whenever I'm feeling anxious or whenever he's having his thoughts.[18]

If you continue talking to and texting friends, they know they can open up to you. Consistent availability shows your support and that you genuinely care about their well-being. However, while checking in regularly is important, you want to do so in a way that is not intrusive or overbearing. You can casually ask how they are doing or other open-ended questions. Additionally, sharing updates about your own life will help them feel it is a mutual conversation. According to David Radar, a psychology graduate from the University of Hertfordshire, regular check-ins can significantly impact someone dealing with stress or mental health issues, helping them feel less isolated and more connected to their support network. "Consistently keeping in touch with friends creates a space for honest conversations, allowing them to express themselves without worrying about being judged,"[19] writes Radar. Your consistent, compassionate presence can make a world of difference in your friends' journey toward better mental health.

> "Consistently keeping in touch with friends creates a space for honest conversations, allowing them to express themselves without worrying about being judged."[19]
>
> —David Radar, psychology graduate and mental health writer

CHAPTER THREE

What Actions Can I Take?

You've seen signs that a friend is struggling, and you've talked with that friend. Now what? First, it's important to remember that you are not responsible for fixing your friends' problems. But you can offer help and support. One of the most important ways to support friends who are going through mental health struggles is simply being there for them. This can be done in many different ways, from being physically present to providing emotional support. Continuing to show them you are invested in their life and are there for them adds to their support system.

A key component of support is to continue to check in and communicate with them after your initial conversation about their mental health. Set up times to meet in person or via text and phone to ensure you are there for them and can see how they are doing. Regular check-ins show friends that you genuinely care and are willing to listen, providing them with a safe space to share their thoughts and emotions. When checking in, give them openings to talk about how they are feeling. Use open-ended questions to help you understand what is going on in their life and how they feel.

Regular check-ins offered significant support to Tiffany's friend, who was sixteen when she lost her mom during the COVID-19 pandemic. During this hard time, Tiffany made a point to talk to her friend regularly, offering a listening ear without pushing her to share more than she was comfortable

> "Engaging in positive, pleasant activities (even when your friend may not be sure they want to!) can boost their mood."[20]
>
> —Lindsay Macchia, associate psychologist at the Child Mind Institute

with. Tiffany also helped her friend by suggesting activities they could do together that provided comfort and distraction, like watching movies, going for walks, or even just sitting together in silence. These actions showed her friend that she wasn't alone in her grief and that Tiffany was there to support her in any way she needed. Lindsay Macchia, an associate psychologist at the Child Mind Institute, notes that such support can help friends dealing with any type of mental health illness or crisis. "Engaging in positive, pleasant activities (even when your friend may not be sure they want to!) can boost their mood," notes Macchia. "Whether anxiety, depression, or another emotion is causing your friend to want to withdraw, getting them to participate in energizing or fun activities is a great way to support them."[20]

Practical Ways to Help

If friends have taken the step to seek outside help, taking them to therapy or doctor appointments can show them they're not alone and can provide them with moral support. Doing this may help reduce the anxiety they might feel about seeking professional help. Sara, in Australia, talked to her boyfriend when she noticed changes in his behavior. After opening up and talking, she realized her boyfriend was struggling with depression and anxiety. She eventually convinced him to see the school counselor. She even took him to his first appointment, since he was nervous about going alone. Since then, he has gone to appointments regularly on his own, and how he feels and deals with his problems has significantly improved.

Mental health struggles can often make it hard to keep up with schoolwork or chores. Another practical way to help may be to offer to complete any chores they normally do, like walking the dog or mowing the yard. In 2022 Talia Bina was struggling with depression while at college. She did not have the energy to clean her room or keep things tidy. A friend came over to study, and before the friend left, without asking she cleaned up the room for Bina. Bina writes:

> She packed her things and then headed over to my desk. She organized everything. She put away my makeup, arranged things in drawers, rearranged everything on my desk, put away the dirty clothes on the chair, and headed over to my dresser to organize everything in a way that left me room to put my laptop on top when I was done using it. She warmed up my Starbucks coffee that had gotten too cold and folded my blankets, leaving the room looking almost perfect.[21]

The mess had been stressing Bina, and her friend gave her some relief with those actions and reminded her that she had support.

Helping with daily tasks, such as dog walking or housecleaning, can be a big support to friends experiencing mental health crises.

Encourage Effort

Obsessive-compulsive disorder (OCD) is a mental health condition characterized by persistent, unwanted thoughts (obsessions) and repetitive behaviors (compulsions). The behaviors, such as knocking on a door a certain number of times every time one goes by it or washing one's hands over and over again, are used to reduce the stress caused by obsessive thoughts.

Teens can help friends with OCD by being patient and understanding that, even with treatment, the compulsions may still occur. Someone with OCD can show improvement one day and experience a setback the next. As a friend, the best way to help is not to point out when the compulsions continue, since this can add pressure and anxiety. However, mental health experts do suggest that one can focus on positive reinforcement. If you see improvement in a friend's compulsions, don't hesitate to point them out. Noticing progress may give your friend hope of eventually managing the condition. Encouraging efforts, rather than focusing on setbacks, helps create a supportive environment as a person works toward managing OCD.

Helping friends with their studies and picking up their assignments if they miss school can also alleviate some of their stress. You could also work with them on assignments if you are in the same class to help them understand any classwork they need to catch up on. This can prevent them from feeling overwhelmed and falling behind.

Another way to help is to organize and participate in activities to help them get out of their thoughts for a bit and focus on something fun. Whether it is playing a sport, watching movies, or just hanging out, these activities can provide stress relief and a break from worrying. Engaging in shared activities can help improve their overall mood and be fun for everyone. During high school and college, Shannon Beveridge experienced much anxiety and even suicidal thoughts as she struggled to understand her sexual identity. Friends reaching out just to hang out was a major help. "I mean, I don't really like talking about my feelings very much so sometimes my friends being there for me was just them sitting on my couch with me and watching Netflix for like hours, and that was enough. Just to remind me that there are people out there who care about me and wanted me to stick around,"[22] Beveridge explains.

Understanding the Issue

Educating yourself about a friend's mental health condition is another way to help. It allows you to familiarize yourself with symptoms and triggers. It can also give you a way to help your friend avoid those triggers.

There are many reliable websites that accurately describe all sorts of mental health conditions. These may be websites affiliated with a well-known medical clinic such as the Mayo Clinic, nonprofit organizations that specialize in mental health such as the Jed Foundation, or government agencies such as the Substance Abuse and Mental Health Services Administration. These sites usually explain what the condition is, how it affects people, and common symptoms, triggers, and treatments. The information found on these sites doesn't necessarily apply to every individual, but it will provide a basic understanding of the problems and challenges experienced by most people who have the condition. It will also give you a clearer picture of what your friend experiences daily.

> "I don't really like talking about my feelings very much so sometimes my friends being there for me was just them sitting on my couch with me and watching Netflix for like hours, and that was enough."[22]
>
> —Shannon Beveridge, teen with anxiety

The effort you make to learn about your friend's condition can smooth the way for conversation. Your friend might already be aware of some of the triggers that set off bouts of anxiety or depression, but now you can discuss those events together. For instance, if a friend experiences social anxiety, you might discuss how going to parties or crowded places leads to heightened anxiety. Together you might be able to come up with ways to avoid situations like this or other situations that have become a problem.

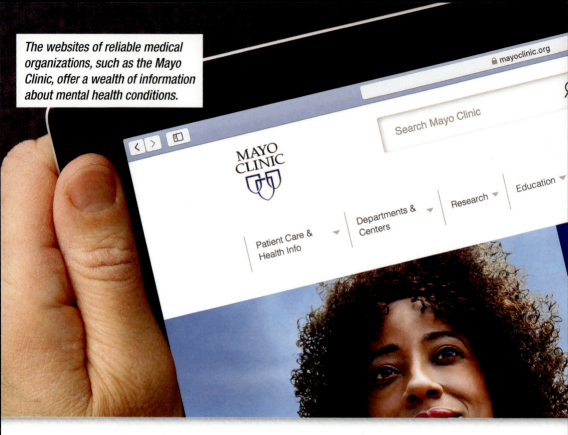

The websites of reliable medical organizations, such as the Mayo Clinic, offer a wealth of information about mental health conditions.

Brainstorming ideas together for how to deal with triggers that can't be avoided is another step. Together, you can develop a plan that outlines specific actions to take when faced with these triggers. For example, if feeling overwhelmed by a crowd, a self-care strategy could be to step outside for fresh air and a short walk. Other ideas might include deep-breathing exercises, listening to calming music, or having a trusted friend to call. By having these strategies in place, your friend can feel more in control when triggers arise.

Catherine is a young woman who obsessively focuses on what she views as flaws or defects in her appearance. She describes how her friend helps steer her away from the triggers that heighten her discomfort:

> You confiscate my phone if you notice I'm taking a selfie, pre-empting the inevitable slide into an endless cycle of taking, deleting and retaking photos of my face. You walk on the inside of the pavement, separating me from the

windows of buildings. In fact, it now only takes seconds for you to recognize my thinking-about-my-face expression and steer me away from whatever reflective surface I've become glued to (oven doors oddly seem to present a particular danger).[23]

This kind of support has helped Catherine in managing the daily challenges of her disorder.

Recognizing the problem is a first step toward helping. Ava Max knew that her friend was hurting as a result of a difficult breakup. She saw her friend starting to spiral into depression. Max noticed her acting oddly—not engaging with friends and staying home by herself in her room. She knew this was a sign of depression and wanted to provide some relief. "She just felt so down after this breakup. It wasn't healthy," Max explains. "So I went inside her room, turned on the lights and was like, 'we're going shopping.'"[24] And while shopping and getting a friend to go out will not cure the problem, it can help lift his or her spirits and provide some relief.

Helping with Social Media

If, in talking to your friend, you realize that social media has become part of the problem, you might be able to help with that too. Although the connections made through social media can be a positive force in people's lives, social media can also be a negative space that hurts emotional well-being. According to a recent advisory from the US surgeon general, social media poses profound risks to the mental health of young people. These risks include increased exposure to cyberbullying, negative social comparisons, and the potential for addictive behaviors. For example, the advisory included the results from a 2022 survey about the impact of social media on a young person's body image. In this survey, 46 percent of adolescents aged thirteen to seventeen said social media makes them feel worse about their bodies. Additionally, a 2021 US Government Accountability Office report suggests that

From Afar

Sometimes anxiety or depression become so crippling that a residential treatment center offers the best hope for recovery. In these centers, patients might not be allowed to use a phone, and visits may be restricted. But friends can still write letters. When Meg Wilder was seventeen, she entered a residential treatment center because she was experiencing crippling anxiety, depression, and suicidal ideation. She was lonely and couldn't use the telephone in her first weeks. "I can't explain the joy, comfort and peace I felt when reading through my letters," Wilder writes. "Mail time soon became a precious and sacred part of my day. The fact that people would take the time to write me a letter shocked me. I didn't think that anyone cared about me. A simple handwritten letter helped me feel valued, loved and important." While it has been years since she was in the treatment center, Wilder says that those letters had a major impact on her recovery. Reaching out in whatever way you can to a friend can provide great comfort.

Meg Wilder, "How Handwritten Letters Helped Me Through Residential Treatment," The Mighty, December 22, 2021. https://themighty.com.

"exposure to online discrimination and hate predicts increases in anxiety and depressive symptoms, even after controlling for how much adolescents are exposed to similar experiences offline."[25]

If you think social media is negatively affecting your friend's mental health, there are several ways to help. One way to bring up the topic of online experiences is to first share your own experiences with social media. Letting a friend know that you too have encountered difficult situations online can help that friend feel validated, understood, and not alone.

If any of your friends are experiencing negative interactions on social media, work together to come up with ways to avoid these harmful areas. This might include blocking individuals who are causing distress, which can prevent exposure to harmful comments and cyberbullying. Additionally, your friends can add more privacy controls to manage who can view and interact with their online posts, reducing the pressure of constant comparison and judgment. Lastly, getting friends to limit how much information they share online helps them manage the amount of feedback they receive, which can reduce feelings of inadequacy or disappointment from lack of engagement. By taking these steps, your friends can create a safer and more positive online environment.

Another effective strategy is to encourage your friends to take regular breaks from social media. According to a 2023 Gallup poll, the average teen spends 4.8 hours a day on social media, and 37 percent spend more than five hours a day on social media. A break, even if only for a few hours a day, can help reduce the constant exposure to potentially negative content. Using this time to instead engage in offline activities can boost mood and self-esteem. This could include activities like reading, exercising, or spending time with family and friends.

Remind your friends that you are available to talk if or when social media interactions turn ugly or become draining. Regularly

Social media makes it all too easy for teens to compare themselves to others. Joyful posts can stand in sharp contrast to someone's own mental health struggles and make things seem worse.

check in so that your friends know you're there for support and to listen. This open line of communication can help people process their feelings and understand that they are not alone in dealing with these issues.

Uplift and Support

From just hanging out with each other to discussing ways to handle social media, friends have much to offer when it comes to helping someone close who is experiencing mental health challenges. Treatments and cures should be left to medical and mental health professionals, but supporting, listening, and talking or even just spending time together are the best ways for one friend to help another.

> "I know that if a friend or family member is depressed, the best thing to do is help them in every way you can, be their friend and hug them a lot, but leave the medical work to the professionals."[26]
>
> —Sara, teen with boyfriend who struggled with depression

Sara, who lives in Australia, was a major help to her boyfriend as he battled depression. She was there for him to talk to, check in with, and hang out with, which ultimately helped him through his issues. "I know that if a friend or family member is depressed, the best thing to do is help them in every way you can, be their friend and hug them a lot, but leave the medical work to the professionals,"[26] Sara explains. By doing so, she had a positive impact on his recovery.

CHAPTER FOUR

Reaching Out for Help

There are times when professional help is needed for a friend dealing with mental health issues. Sometimes people who are struggling recognize this need. Often, they don't. In extreme situations, you may need to seek immediate help for someone, even if he or she does not consent. Always err on the side of caution when it comes to mental health.

Asking for Help

Sometimes people realize they need help. If they ask you to assist in finding it, take that request seriously. The first step is to validate their decision to ask for help. Let them know you see this as an important and positive action on their part. It's often difficult to overcome the stigma that still exists over seeking mental health help. Showing your support for the decision can help them overcome any worries they have about seeking professional assistance.

Once you've supported their decision, talk about the various resources available. If you are unsure, you can do some research together. You may want to start looking at the websites of accredited mental health organizations. Organizations such as the National Alliance on Mental Illness, Mental Health America, and the National Institute of Mental Health offer professionally approved information and resources. School websites often include the names and contact information for school counselors, who can also be a resource.

Encourage a friend in crisis to explore these options and see which might feel most comfortable and accessible to them. Doing this with you may help your friend find the process less intimidating. After finding information, it's important to urge your friend to contact at least one of these resources—by email, by phone, or in person. You could be present when your friend makes that first call. You could help your friend compose that first email. You could even go with your friend to that first in-person visit. Sometimes, taking that first step can be scary, and having a friend nearby can make all the difference. By encouraging action, you help your friend transition from thinking about getting help to actually getting it. Being a consistent source of support can help friends feel more secure in their decision to seek help.

When You See It and They Don't

Admitting you need help is not easy for some people. Even though you might realize the need for outside help, your friend might not see it. This can be a challenging situation, but your voice can make a significant difference. If this happens, approach the situation with care.

> "Remind your friend that seeking help for their mental health is a sign of strength."[27]
>
> —The Jed Foundation, a nonprofit mental health organization

Start with an open and honest conversation. Approach your friend with genuine concern and explain why you believe the friend could benefit from outside help. Be gentle in your approach and focus on expressing your concern rather than making your friend feel judged or pressured. The Jed Foundation provides the following suggestions:

> Remind your friend that seeking help for their mental health is a sign of strength. Addressing a problem before it gets worse takes courage and discipline. And it makes sense to seek professional help for something we do not naturally know a lot about or cannot figure out on our own. If it helps, you can liken it to visiting a doctor for a physical . . . working with a coach to improve their athletic ability, or getting a tutor when struggling with a subject in school.[27]

If a friend asks for your help in finding mental health resources, the internet is a good place to start. Check out accredited mental health organizations or your school's website.

By providing specific resources, you can show your friend that it's not difficult to take a step toward getting help. If you or someone you know has ever sought help, share that story, although do not disclose the other person's name without permission.

Sara found herself in uncharted waters when she noticed that her boyfriend was struggling. Although normally upbeat, he started coming across as deeply sad even to the point of crying. At first she tried to support him on her own, but she realized that he needed help that she couldn't provide. "I went and spoke to my dad, who is a youth worker, the next day. He told me all about depression and gave me some numbers that my boyfriend could call," Sara recalls. "Of course, my boyfriend refused to call the counselor, but it cheered him up a little when I told him about the causes of depression. He started to realize it was quite a normal thing."[28] The two

Help for LGBTQ Teens

Studies show that LGBTQ young people are at higher risk than other groups for mental health difficulties. According to the Centers for Disease Control and Prevention, LGBTQ youth are particularly vulnerable due to nonacceptance by others or lack of a supportive community. With specific issues such as coming out, bullying, and understanding their own identity, it can be helpful to use mental health resources that are targeted for LGBTQ teens. One of the most well-known is the Trevor Project. The Trevor Project offers a safe and confidential space where LGBTQ teens can talk to trained counselors around the clock through the Trevor Lifeline at 1-866-488-7386 or through TrevorText and TrevorChat. These services are free and always available, so if your friend needs someone to talk to, this is a good resource.

talked some more. Eventually, Sara's boyfriend agreed to see the school counselor. Although he was unsure at first, Sara's honesty and persistence helped him understand the importance of seeking help. He then started his journey toward recovery.

Need for Immediate Action

In situations when a friend needs immediate help, it's crucial to act quickly. If your friend shows any signs of a mental health crisis, it's essential to seek outside help immediately. These signs can include constant sadness, evidence of self-harm like cuts or burns on the arms or legs, shared thoughts of self-harm or suicide, difficulty functioning in daily activities, or increased use of drugs or alcohol.

People do sometimes feel sad, but persistent feelings of sadness or hopelessness are not just a phase. This can be a sign that someone is struggling with serious issues, including thoughts of suicide or self-harm. If your friend always seems gloomy, talks about feeling worthless, or withdraws from social activities, that's typically not normal teenage moodiness. For example, if your friend has always been passionate about soccer and suddenly stops attending practices, that might be a sign that something else is going on and that your friend needs help to deal with these emotions.

Evidence of self-harm, such as cutting, is another serious sign that immediate help is needed. Helena describes how she benefited from intervention by her friends. A resident of the United Kingdom, she transferred to a new school at about age thirteen after being sexually abused by a teacher. She made friends at the new school. However, she had never fully processed what had happened to her. Because of this her despair intensified. She began cutting and burning herself. Helena's friends noticed her self-harm, and their intervention led her to get the help she needed. "After a year at the school, my friends noticed something was wrong and approached the headteacher to seek help for me," Helena writes. "I had been hurting myself completely in secret—no one had ever seen it before."[29] While it took years of therapy, that intervention helped her achieve emotional stability, and recently, in her early twenties, she graduated from college.

> "I had been hurting myself completely in secret—no one had ever seen it before."[29]
>
> —Helena, teen who had been cutting and burning herself

Persistent feelings of sadness or hopelessness are not just a phase. If a friend displays these symptoms, seek outside help immediately.

Warning signs can occur in the form of words or actions—or sometimes both. Comments about suicide or feeling trapped or like a burden to others should be viewed as warning signs. Actions can also signal a need for help, although they might be more subtle. If a friend starts giving away belongings or saying things like "I won't need this anymore," this too could be a warning sign.

What to Do?

In all of these cases, it's essential to act quickly. If you are in the room, stay by your friend's side. If you are not physically present, call or text to keep in contact. It's okay to ask a direct question to find out whether the friend is contemplating suicide. Once you ask, listen actively. If your friend expresses suicidal thoughts while communicating with you, whether in person or via phone, contact a crisis hotline that can provide immediate assistance and advice. 988 is the number for the Suicide & Crisis Lifeline. Funded by the Substance Abuse and Mental Health Services Administration,

SAMHSA's 988 Suicide & Crisis Lifeline is a 24/7 resource that connects callers to a national network of crisis centers.

Online Signs

Changes in online behavior sometimes speak as loudly as changes you see in person. Cryptic or alarming posts like "I can't take this anymore" or "I wish I could just disappear," sharing pictures of self-injury, or online expressions of hopelessness and despair should not be ignored. And if a normally social friend withdraws suddenly from online interactions or shows abrupt changes in the tone or content of online posts, it could be cause for concern. Another sign is if someone posts negative or highly critical comments about oneself or life in general. If you see these types of actions online, try reaching out to the person to express your concern.

988 connects individuals via voice or text to a national network of local crisis centers. It offers free and confidential emotional support around the clock to those in suicidal crisis or emotional distress in the United States. This hotline is staffed by trained professionals who can offer support and guidance during emergencies.

When you call or text 988, crisis counselors typically provide immediate support, first listening to your concerns and then offering guidance on how to help your friend. Counselors may inquire about your friend's behavior and the signs you have seen that suggest emotional struggle. Based on this information, they may advise you to stay with your friend while you contact 911 emergency services for assistance. Or they might provide resources for local mental health services. Counselors will also offer you support and coping resources to manage the situation and ensure your well-being.

If you cannot contact a crisis center, call 911 for emergency services. Inform the 911 operator of your friend's location and the nature of the concern so the operator can dispatch immediate assistance. Stay in contact with your friend until you are certain they are safe.

Recognizing signs of immediate need and taking action, as Quinn Brightbill did as a junior at Medina High School in Ohio in 2023, can save lives. Trained in mental health aid at school, Brightbill recognized the seriousness of an alarming message from a

> "A lot of people knew I was struggling. A lot of people knew I wasn't OK. But you were the person who made the phone call."[31]
>
> —Christa Marie, who attempted suicide

friend in a group chat. "As soon as I received that note, I knew they were in danger of hurting themselves,"[30] Brightbill recalls. She immediately called the suicide hotline, and her friend is alive today, demonstrating that quick action can save lives.

Calling a friend's or your own parents, or another trusted adult, is another critical step in a crisis. In emergency situations, involving a responsible adult is often necessary. However, consider the context carefully. If you are aware that a friend's parents contribute to his or her mental health issues, it may be more appropriate to reach out to another trusted adult or a professional.

Saving a Life

No matter how you realize a friend needs professional help, the key is to act on that realization promptly. Taking swift action can lead to a healthier emotional place and potentially save that person's life. Christa Marie has fought depression since she was a teen. She shares her story on the Mighty, a website dedicated to health. On this site she posted a letter to a friend who she says saved her from overdosing on pills and ending her life. "A lot of people knew I was struggling. A lot of people knew I wasn't OK. But you were the person who made the phone call. You were the person who stepped in," she writes. "You were the person who cared enough to do something. You are the reason I didn't die that night. You are also one of [the] many reasons I'm still alive today."[31] Physically, she recovered quickly, but this led to more intense therapy and help. Christa Marie believes she wouldn't be alive without her friend's intervention and continued support afterward.

Helping your friends with mental health issues involves being a source of support and guiding them toward necessary resources. Whether your friends ask for help or you recognize they need it, affirm their feelings, provide resources, and encourage action. In immediate need situations, swift and decisive action can make all the difference and potentially save a life.

CHAPTER FIVE

Taking Care of Yourself While Helping Others

Young people can offer support to friends who are struggling, but they are not responsible for fixing the problems a friend may be experiencing. The best thing a teen can do is to listen, talk, and urge that friend to reach out for professional help. Getting so caught up in a friend's problems that it affects your own metal health does not help your friend, and it is not good for you.

It is important to be mindful of how you are being affected by helping a friend. "Supporting others can be mentally and emotionally exhausting," explains Megan Bruneau, a registered clinical counselor. "Often, we find ourselves focusing all our energy on our friend or loved one, and we wind up neglecting ourselves in the process."[32] It is worth remembering that you cannot help someone else if you do not maintain your own emotional health.

> "Supporting others can be mentally and emotionally exhausting."[32]
>
> —Megan Bruneau, a registered clinical counselor

Emotional Burden and Consequences

When determining how well you are coping emotionally with your efforts to help a friend, look to yourself for some common effects. One of the most common effects of becoming too involved in a friend's mental health journey is empathy fatigue. Empathy fatigue, a state of exhaustion and emotional withdrawal, can result from prolonged exposure to situations that require empathy, such as a friend's crisis.

Empathy fatigue can have both physical and emotional effects. Feeling emotionally drained or overwhelmed, numbness to a friend's suffering, irritability, and even physical symptoms like headaches and stomachaches are common signs. Psychologist Susan Albers describes some of the most common symptoms she sees in patients who are experiencing empathy fatigue:

> Some of the physical signs are difficulty sleeping. . . . You can't turn your brain off. . . . Sometimes there's a lot of GI [gastrointestinal] problems because you have a lot of stress, upset stomach. You may feel exhausted all the time. I work with a lot of people who experience emotional eating as well. So they may experience some extreme changes in their eating. Also isolation, that they come home and they go in their bedroom and shut the door because they just can't handle any more stuff.[33]

Empathy fatigue can occur when someone is overly invested in how someone else is coping. Nurses, counselors, and those in professions in which they care for people with any kind of trauma are particularly at risk for this, as are those who are helping someone close to them. "[Empathy fatigue] is the emotional and physical exhaustion that happens from caring for people day, after day, after day," explains Albers. "Over time . . . what we see is that people experience a sense of numbness or distancing or difficulty . . . caring."[34] She explains that empathy fatigue is a defense mechanism. Pay attention to the symptoms,

> "[Empathy fatigue] is the emotional and physical exhaustion that happens from caring for people day, after day, after day."[34]
>
> —Susan Albers, psychologist

Empathy fatigue is not just psychological. It can lead to stress-related physical symptoms, including headache and stomachaches.

emotional and physical, as they are telling you that you need to be mindful of your own emotional well-being.

Not doing this can lead to problems. For example, Elaine Russell was determined to be there for her friend who was cutting and had been hospitalized as a result. When her friend was back at school, Russell would check in with her every day to see whether she was cutting. Russell felt it was her job to ensure that her friend did not cut again. She was constantly checking on her friend and made herself always available to the friend. Unfortunately, her friend continued to cut. Russell worried so much about her friend that she neglected her own needs, and as a result, her own mental health began to suffer. Her grades dropped, she was not getting enough sleep, and she became withdrawn. "At one point, I began to cut myself because I knew she was not getting better and I had convinced myself that it was my fault,"[35] Russell explains. Russell's parents noticed the changes in her and that the friend had become the only focus in her life. They intervened

Feeling Thankful for Good Friends

Marie Minerva Estela had a rough first year of college. She was dealing with severe depression and manic episodes. The challenges she was experiencing spilled over into the lives of her roommates. Estela realized she needed to act. She took a year off school and got professional help. When she returned to school, she continued with counseling and medical treatment. Both enabled her to function better and develop friendships with new roommates. However, even with treatment and counseling, she experienced occasional depressive episodes. Her roommates, who are still her friends years later, supported her during this time. "When these roommates . . . gave their bridesmaid speeches at my wedding, they all cried. I didn't cry. I laughed, because I was happy that I had good friends who'd extended generosity to me over and over when I lived with them. Who knows why we earn the grace of our friends. My life would be worse without it." Now, looking back, Estela appreciates the complexities her roommates faced and the support they gave.

Marie Minerva Estela, "Are You the 'Troubled Roommate' at College? I Was," The Mighty, February 20, 2023. https://themighty.com.

and got Russell help. Through therapy, she improved and realized how severely she was affected by becoming so entrenched in her friend's problems.

Setting Boundaries

While recognizing the signs of empathy fatigue is important, even more crucial is knowing how to prevent it or alleviate it. Therapists emphasize that it is crucial to set boundaries with your friend regarding what you can do for them and how you can be there for them. Doing this will allow you to maintain your mental health while still being a support to your friend.

Setting boundaries is not easy. It requires first determining for yourself what you can handle in terms of assisting your friend. Without clear boundaries, the lines between your friend's emotions and your own can become blurred, leading to increased stress and potential burnout. When setting boundaries, start by making a list of what you can and cannot handle. This could involve setting limits on the amount of time you spend with your friend in person, how often you talk on the phone, and even the amount of texting you do. It can even include what you talk about. For example, you might decide that you can only deal with one phone call a day and that certain topics are off-limits because they are triggering for you.

The next step is to communicate your boundaries clearly and honestly to your friend. Set up a time and place to meet that allows you both to feel at ease. When you talk, do not criticize your friend or his or her actions. Instead, use "I" statements to express your needs without blaming or accusing them. For example, you could say, "I need a day to recharge after we talk because it can be emotionally draining for me," instead of "You are stressing me out with your issues."

Once you and your friend have established boundaries, it's important to abide by them. Consistency reinforces the boundaries you've set and prevents misunderstandings. Consistency also demonstrates respect for your own needs and encourages your friend to respect them as well.

When you've achieved this, you still need to check in with yourself regularly to monitor how you're feeling emotionally and physically. If you are still feeling overwhelmed, you can readjust the boundaries. The Jed Foundation states:

> It's also okay if how you show up for your friend changes over time. For example, you might be willing to give more time and energy when your friend is experiencing a crisis, but as the crisis resolves, your friend might not need the same level of support—or may need mental health support that you can't provide. Or if you've been actively supporting a friend and something happens in your life that requires more time and attention, you may need to step back from helping your friend to take care of yourself. It's important to continue to be honest with your friend about how much you can give.[36]

Relax and Recharge

At any time in life, self-care is important for one's mental health. When helping another who is struggling, it is even more important to monitor and care for yourself. While setting boundaries with friends is a good way to protect your emotional health, there are many other ways to also care for yourself.

During each day, allow time for activities that help you relax and recharge. This could be reading a book, exercising, gardening, cooking, playing a musical instrument, or spending time in nature. Even ten minutes a day can reenergize most people. For example, after an intense discussion with a friend, it may help you to take a bike ride in your neighborhood or paint a picture. "Set aside dedicated time each day to do something that makes you feel calm, alleviates stress, or simply makes you happy—whether

Helping others can be an emotional and physical drain. Getting regular exercise is a proven way to recharge and relax.

Helping a Friend Can Help You

Establishing boundaries is important when dealing with a friend who is experiencing challenges in his or her life. But being friends with someone who is depressed or experiencing other issues doesn't have to always be hard. You can still have fun together and share meaningful conversations. According to Caroline Leaf, a clinical psychologist, "Talking to friends with depression can be surprisingly easy and enjoyable. It's not about flashy, Instagram-worthy moments but rather the kind of fun where you simply enjoy each other's company without pressure or judgment."

Helping friends has also been found to be beneficial to your own emotional well-being. "Helping others can also increase our own healing by up to 63%!" Leaf says. "This is why it is so important to try to be there for a friend who is experiencing mental distress." While it's important to monitor and care for your own mental state, remember that helping a friend can also uplift you.

Quoted in Randi Mazzella, "Friendship and Depression: How to Support a Friend Who's in Emotional Pain," HealthCentral, October 17, 2022. www.healthcentral.com.

---

it's meditation, giving yourself a facial, cooking, dancing to your favorite playlist, walking your dog, or doodling in a coloring book,"[37] recommends Seize the Awkward.

Jonathan, who volunteered with a teen helpline when he was a high school sophomore, found it necessary to decompress after helping peers with problems. Because he knew it was easy to become emotionally overinvested when working with so many in need, he created a plan for staying grounded. Speaking in 2020 while doing this work, he said, "Some things I do for self-care are going outside for walks, going for a longboard ride, and listening to music."[38]

Care for Yourself First

Even when you take steps to care for yourself, helping and supporting friends who are struggling can leave you feeling overwhelmed. If this happens, try talking to a friend or family member or other trusted adult—someone who can help you gain outside perspective. Talking to a health professional might also be worthwhile. A key to taking care of yourself when helping others is to continually assess how you are feeling and take actions as needed. Randy Auerbach, associate professor of psychiatry at Columbia University, explains:

> If you see a friend or classmate struggling with depression, it could be really overwhelming. It could be that it triggers sadness, worry, or exasperation. And if that's the case, you should take stock of how it's affecting you and also seek out help or guidance on how to manage these uncomfortable feelings.[39]

Wherever you are on your journey with being there for a friend or peer, take stock of how you are personally feeling.

Counseling can provide much needed help and support for teens who are experiencing mental health crises.

After Elaine Russell's parents discovered she was cutting, they got her professional help. Therapy is what led to her realization that she needed to care for her own mental health needs even when being there for a friend. She acknowledged that she had become extremely stressed and anxious herself, since her sole focus had become "saving" her friend. With therapy, Russell learned to set boundaries with her friend, which included a period of distance. As a result, her mental health improved. At the same time, so did the mental health of her friend, who had become too dependent on Russell. Without being able to constantly text and talk to Russell, her friend could focus more on getting professional help. Russell says she learned a valuable lesson from the experience. She spoke about it on a TED Talk. "The best thing you can do to help your friends is to help yourself," Russell explains. "Before even looking at what was best for my friend, I needed to ensure that I was in a safe space to offer my support without getting too drawn in . . . with proper awareness and strength you can support your friends."[40] Russell's experience shows the importance of prioritizing self-care and setting boundaries when supporting friends. If you are taking care of yourself, then you will be able to give your friends meaningful support.

> "The best thing you can do to help your friends is to help yourself."[40]
>
> —Elaine Russell, teen whose friend suffered from depression and cutting

SOURCE NOTES

Introduction: Teens in Crisis

1. Quoted in Children's Health, "How Teens Can Help Friends with Anxiety and Depression," 2024. www.childrens.com.
2. Quoted in Reachout, "Stories from Young People with Depression," 2024. https://au.reachout.com.
3. Quoted in Yahoo! News, "Amid Mental Health Crisis, School Districts Are Bringing In Therapists to Counsel Students," July 7, 2023. www.yahoo.com.

Chapter One: How Do I Recognize a Mental Health Crisis?

4. Elaine Russell, "What Trying to Help My Friend Taught Me About Mental Health," Facebook, May 3, 2019. www.facebook.com.
5. Claire McCarthy, "The Mental Health Crisis Among Children and Teens: How Parents Can Help," Harvard Health Publishing, March 8, 2022. www.health.harvard.edu.
6. Quoted in Savannah Tomei, "Hope Squads at Elmbrook," Spectrum News, March 20, 2024. https://spectrumnews1.com.
7. Daneisha Carter, "Finding Light at the End of the Tunnel," Anxiety & Depression Association of America, August 31, 2023. https://adaa.org.
8. Quoted in Tomei, "Hope Squads at Elmbrook."
9. Quoted in Mind, "Signs My Friend or Partner May Be Struggling," 2024. www.mind.org.uk.
10. Quoted in Anya Kamenetz, "A Surprising Remedy for Teens in Mental Health Crises," MinnPost, May 17, 2023. www.minnpost.com.

Chapter Two: Talking and Listening

11. Quoted in Kamenetz, "A Surprising Remedy for Teens in Mental Health Crises."
12. Quoted in Catherine Gewertz, "Students Train to Spot Peers with Mental Health Struggles and Guide Them to Help," Education Week, March 1, 2022. www.edweek.org.
13. Quoted in Student Spotlight, "'Hope Squad' Helps Students with Mental Health," PBS, September 13, 2022. www.pbs.org.
14. Brené Brown, "Brené Brown: What Is Empathy?," Boulder Crest, September 13, 2023. https://bouldercrest.org.

15. Kathryn Gordon, "How to Help a Friend Through a Tough Time, According to a Clinical Psychologist," Vox, December 10, 2019. www.vox.com.
16. Remi Cruz, "Remi Cruz on Trusting Your Gut," Seize the Awkward, 2020. https://seizetheawkward.org.
17. Cruz, "Remi Cruz on Trusting Your Gut."
18. Liza Koshy, "Liza Koshy on Opening Up," Seize the Awkward, 2020. https://seizetheawkward.org.
19. David Radar, "How Checking Up on Friends Supports Mental Health," Psychreg, March 20, 2024. www.psychreg.org.

Chapter Three: What Actions Can I Take?

20. Quoted in Katherine Martinelli, "How to Support a Friend with Mental Health Challenges," Child Mind Institute, October 30, 2023. https://childmind.org.
21. Talia Bina, "How My Friend Cleaning My Room Helped My Depression," The Mighty, November 9, 2022. https://themighty.com.
22. Shannon Beveridge, "Shannon Beveridge on Being There," Seize the Awkward, 2020. https://seizetheawkward.org.
23. Catherine, "Friendship and Body Dysmorphic Disorder," The Mind, April 10, 2020. www.mind.org.uk.
24. Ava Max, "Ava Max on Mental Health and Friendship," Seize the Awkward, 2020. https://seizetheawkward.org.
25. Quoted in Diane Graber, "New Health Advisory on Teen Social Media Use," *Raising Humans in a Digital World* (blog), *Psychology Today*, May 10, 2023. www.psychologytoday.com.
26. Sara, "Sara's Experience Helping Her Boyfriend Overcome Depression," Reachout, 2024. https://au.reachout.com.

Chapter Four: Reaching Out for Help

27. Jed Foundation, "How and When to Help a Friend Reach Out for Support." https://jedfoundation.org.
28. Sara, "Sara's Experience Helping Her Boyfriend Overcome Depression."
29. Quoted in Childline, "Self-Harm: Helena's Story." www.childline.org.uk.
30. Quoted in Nichole Vrsansky, "Northeast Ohio Students Opening Conversation for Preventing Teen Suicide," Cleveland 19 News, December 21, 2023. www.cleveland19.com.
31. Christa Marie, "To the Friend Who Saved My Life When I Attempted Suicide," The Mighty, November 9. 2022. https://themighty.com.

Chapter Five: Taking Care of Yourself While Helping Others

32. Megan Bruneau, "9 Ways to Help a Depressed Friend (Without Getting Drained)," Mind Body Green, March 25, 2020. www.mindbodygreen.com.
33. Quoted in Cleveland Clinic, "Are You Experiencing Empathy Fatigue? With Dr. Susan Albers," October 28, 2019. https://my.clevelandclinic.org.
34. Quoted in Cleveland Clinic, "Are You Experiencing Empathy Fatigue?"
35. Russell, "What Trying to Help My Friend Taught Me About Mental Health."
36. Jed Foundation, "How to Take Care of Yourself When You're Taking Care of Friends." https://jedfoundation.org.
37. Seize the Awkward, "Taking Care of Your Own Mental Health," 2020. https://seizetheawkward.org.
38. Quoted in Teenline, *Jonathon's Self-Care Tip*, YouTube, 2020. www.youtube.com/watch?v=oi1Da39wQPI.
39. Quoted in Columbia Psychiatry, *Helping a Friend Struggling with Depression: Tips from Dr. Randy Auerbach*, YouTube, 2019. www.youtube.com/watch?v=cYjwcUulnCc.
40. Russell, "What Trying to Help My Friend Taught Me About Mental Health."

GETTING HELP AND INFORMATION

Books

Stacey Freedenthall, *Loving Someone with Suicidal Thoughts: What Family, Friends, and Partners Can Say and Do*. Oakland, CA: New Harbinger, 2023.

Michael Hollander, *Helping Teens Who Cut: Using DBT Skills to End Self-Injury*. Ashland, OR: Blackstone, 2023.

Teen Thrive, *The Anxiety Toolkit for Teens: Easy and Practical CBT and DBT Tools to Manage your Stress Anxiety Worry and Panic*. Teen Thrive, 2022.

Teen Thrive, *The DBT Skills Workbook for Teens: A Fun Guide to Manage Anxiety and Stress, Understand Your Emotions and Learn Effective Communication Skills*. Teen Thrive, 2021.

Internet Sources

Micah Abraham, "12 Do's and Don'ts of Helping Someone with Anxiety," Calm Clinic, February 12, 2021. www.calmclinic.com.

BBC, "How to Help a Friend Who's Struggling with Mental Health," September 24, 2018. www.bbc.com.

Mayo Clinic, "Teen Depression," August 12, 2022. www.mayoclinic.org.

Mental Health Literacy, "Understanding Self Injury/Self Harm," 2024. https://mentalhealthliteracy.org.

The Mind, "Tips for Supporting Your Friends or Partner(s)—for 11–18 Year Olds," 2023. www.mind.org.uk.

National Institute of Mental Health, "5 Actions for Helping Someone in Emotional Pain," 2022. www.nimh.nih.gov.

Psych Central, "How to Help a Friend with an Eating Disorder," April 25, 2022. https://psychcentral.com.

Suicide Call Back, "Six Signs My Friend Is Depressed (and How I Can Help)." www.suicidecallbackservice.org.au.

Ada Tseng and Claire Hannah Collins, "Peer Support Can Help People with Mental Health Challenges. Here's How It Works," *Los Angeles Times*, October 4, 2021. www.latimes.com.

Organizations and Websites

Child Mind Institute
www.childmind.org
The Child Mind Institute offers resources for understanding mental health issues that affect children and adolescents. Visitors can find articles, videos, and guides on supporting friends with mental health challenges, as well how to manage their own mental well-being.

Jed Foundation
www.jedfoundation.org
The Jed Foundation focuses on protecting emotional health and preventing suicide among teens and young adults. Its website provides resources for students on ways to support friends in distress, how to cope with their own mental health challenges, and ways to connect with mental health professionals.

National Alliance on Mental Illness (NAMI)
www.nami.org
NAMI provides information on different mental health conditions, treatment options, and coping strategies. Visitors can find guides on how to talk to friends about mental health, recognize warning signs, and encourage peers to seek help.

988 Suicide & Crisis Lifeline
https://988lifeline.org
This website is dedicated to suicide prevention and support of individuals in crisis. It offers a confidential helpline service available around the clock for those in need of immediate assistance. The crisis line can be reached through call, text, or chat.

ReachOut
https://au.reachout.com
ReachOut provides mental health support and information to young people. The site features personal stories, online access to peer support, and practical advice on how to help friends dealing with mental health issues, as well as how to seek help for oneself.

Seize the Awkward

www.seizetheawkward.org

Seize the Awkward is an organization that encourages young people to have conversations about mental health with their friends. It provides conversation starters with friends, tips for supporting friends, and personal stories from youths about their mental health journeys.

Mental Health Literacy

https://mentalhealthliteracy.org

This organization provides information on various mental health disorders, how to manage mental health, and videos of people who have struggled with mental health. It also has a youth advisory council whose focus is to help develop mental health materials, projects, and initiatives targeted at youth.

INDEX

Note: Boldface page numbers indicate illustrations.

academic expectations, as contributing factor in teens' mental health crisis, 5
Albers, Susan, 46
American Psychiatric Association, 16
American Psychological Association, 11
American School Counselor Association, 5
anxiety disorders, signs of, 10, 11
Auerbach, Randy, 52

behavioral changes
   length of, and intervention, 14
   peers' ability to notice, 6, 7
   as signs of mental health crisis, 8, 11–13, 33
Beveridge, Shannon, 30–31
Bina, Talia, 28–29
Black teenagers, increase in mental health crises in, 4
Brightbill, Quinn, 43–44
Brown, Brené, 20
Bruneau, Megan, 45

Carter, Daneisha, 12
Centers for Disease Control and Prevention (CDC), 4, 8, 40

Clark High School (Nevada), 19
confidentiality, 21
COVID-19 pandemic, 5
Cruz, Remi, 23–25, **24**
cutting, as sign of mental health crisis, 8

Davis, Suzanna, 18
depression, signs of, 11, 33
Devine, Cooper, 13

eating disorders, signs of, 10
empathy, 20–21
empathy fatigue, 46–49, **47**
Estela, Marie Minerva, 48

Gallup polls, 35
Gordon, Kathryn, 23
Gorman, Janie, 15–16
Grant Us Hope, 18

Harju, Izabella, 19
hopelessness, number of teens experiencing persistent, 4, 8
Hope Squad, 13, 18

Jed Foundation
   on peer intervention boundaries, 49
   following instincts, 12
   helping friends find treatment, 38
   as resource, 31, 58

Koshy, Liza, 25–26

Leaf, Caroline, 51
LGBTQ teenagers, 4, 40

Macchia, Lindsay, 28
Max, Ava, 33
Mayo Clinic, 31, **32**
McCarthy, Claire, 9
Mental Health America, 37
mental health conditions, learning about, 31
mental health crisis
  basic facts about, 8–9
  increase in number of teens having, 4
  signs of
    ability of friends to notice, 6, 7
    changes in online behavior, 43
    contemplating suicide, 18–19
    cutting, 8
    immediate action needed, 40–42, 44
    keeping to self, 33
    nonverbal clues, 14–15, **15**
    physical, 9–11, 16
    verbal clues, 14
    weight changes, 10
  social media and, 4–5, 15, 33–34, **35**, 43
Mighty (website), 44
Mind, 15
Murthy, Vivek, 9

National Alliance on Mental Illness (NAMI), 17, 37, 58
National Council for Mental Wellbeing, 7
National Institute of Mental Health, 37
988 Suicide & Crisis Lifeline, **42**, 42–43, 58
nonjudgmental, being, 21
nonverbal language, 21

obsessive-compulsive disorder (OCD), 30

panic attacks, signs of, 16
peer intervention
  ability to confide in friends and, 5, 6, **6**, 17
  importance of, 5, 6–7, 16
  intervenor
    attitudes of, 19–21
    boundaries set by, 48–49, 53
    consequences for, 46–49, **47**
    helping others helps, 51
    mental health self-care, **50**, 50–52
  training for, 13, 18, **18**
  knowing when to initiate
    actions to take when faced with triggers, 32–33
    noticing behavioral changes and, 6
    signs of immediate action being needed, 40–42, 44
    trusting instincts and, 12, 23–25
  location for, 22, **22**, 23
  online, 20
  tips
    conversation starters, 22

finding treatment, 37–38, **39**, 39–40
handwritten letters, 34
hanging out, 30–31
helping with chores, 28–29, **29**
helping with schoolwork, 30
keeping communication open, 25–26, 27–28, 36
morale boosters, 28
open-ended and follow-up questions and, 23
positive reinforcement, 30
personal hygiene, changes in, 13
physical symptoms, without apparent cause, 11, 16
Plater-Zyberk, Helena, 20

Radar, David, 26
Ramsey High School (Ramsey, NJ), 16
ReachOut, 11, 58
reflective listening, 21
residential treatment centers, 34
resources
  books, 57
  988 Suicide & Crisis Lifeline, **42**, 42–43
  organizations, 31, 37, 58
  school mental health support courses, 7, 13, 16, 18
  websites, 44, 57, 58–59
Russell, Elaine, 8, 47–48, 53

sadness, number of teens experiencing persistent, 4, 8
schools
  shortage of counselors, 5
  teaching mental health first aid in, 7, 13, 16, 18
Schulenberg, Lily, 7
Seize the Awkward, 23, 51, 59
self-harm, signs of, 41
Simpson, Vanessa, 6
sleep pattern changes, 11
social media
  average time teenagers spend on, 35
  avoiding harmful effects of, 34–35
  as contributing factor in teens' mental health crisis, 4–5, 33–34, **35**
  signs on, of mental health crisis, 15, 43
Streeby, Kolby, 17
stress, severe, signs of, 10
Substance Abuse and Mental Health Services Administration, 31, **42**, 42–43
suicide
  Hope Squad and, 13, 18
  988 Suicide & Crisis Lifeline, **42**, 42–43
  number of teenagers attempting, 4, 9
  number of teenagers contemplating attempting, 4
  signs of contemplating, 18–19
Supportiv, 20

teenagers
  average time spent on social media by, 35
  body image of, 32, 33–34

increase in number of, having
  mental health crisis, 4
learning about mental health
  conditions, 31
trusting own instincts, 12, 23–25
See also peer intervention
Teen Mental Health First Aid
  course, 16
treatment
  counseling, **52**
  helping friend find, 37–38, **39**,
    39–40

residential centers for,
  34
Trevor Project, 40
triggers, actions to take when
  faced with, 32–33

UnitedHealthcare, 20
US Government Accountability
  Office, 33–34

weight changes, 10
Wilder, Meg, 34

PICTURE CREDITS

Cover: Juanmonino/iStock

6: Antonio Guillem/Shutterstock
10: Antonio Guillem/Shutterstock
13: PeopleImages.com - Yuri A/Shutterstock
15: MDV Edwards/Shutterstock
18: SeventyFour/Shutterstock
22: Motortion Films/Shutterstock
24: OConnor/AFF-USA.com/MEGA/Newscom/TALOS/Newscom
29: LightField Studios/Shutterstock
32: True Images/Alamy Stock Photo
35: Grey Zome/Shutterstock
39: Daniel Hoz/Shutterstock
41: Antonio Guillem/Shutterstock
42: Deutschlandreform/Shutterstock
47: fizkes/Shutterstock
50: Monkey Business Images/Shutterstock
52: fizkes/Shutterstock

ABOUT THE AUTHOR

Leanne Currie-McGhee lives in Norfolk, Virginia, with her husband, Keith; daughters, Grace and Sol; and dog, Delilah. She has been writing books for over two decades.